OCEAN
HABITATS

Written by
Alex Hall

Ocean © 2024 BookLife Publishing
This edition is published by arrangement with BookLife Publishing

sales@northstareditions.com
888-417-0195

979-8-89359-376-1 (epub)
979-8-89359-349-5 (hosted ebook)

Printed in the United States of America
Mankato, MN
092025

American adaptation copyright © 2026 by North Star Editions, Mendota Heights, MN 55120. All rights reserved. No part of this book may be reproduced or utilized in any form or by any means without written permission from the publisher.

Library of Congress Control Number:
The Library of Congress Control Number is available on the Library of Congress website.

ISBN
979-8-89359-319-8 (library bound)
979-8-89359-403-4 (paperback)

Written by:
Alex Hall

Edited by:
Noah Leatherland

Designed by:
Jasmine Pointer

All facts, statistics, web addresses and URLs in this book were verified as valid and accurate at time of writing. No responsibility for any changes to external websites or references can be accepted by either the author or publisher.

Image Credits

All images are courtesy of Shutterstock.com. With thanks to Getty Images, Thinkstock Photo and iStockphoto.

Cover – alazur, Alfmaler, GN.Studio, YG Studio. Throughout – Your Local Llamacorn, alazur, GN.Studio. 4–5 – Himanshu Saraf, Martin Mecnarowski, ChameleonsEye, PHOTO JUNCTION. 6–7 – Myroslava Bozhko, Mozgova. 8–9 – MrVettore, georgieswanderlust, Oleg Kovtun Hydrobio, FtLaud, Quang Vinh Tran, GreenSkyStudio. 10–11 – Kuttelvaserova Stuchelova, Irina Markova, Kim_Briers. 12–13 – Alfmaler, Laverne Nash, Achimdiver. 14–15 – Apolinariy, Tory Kallman. 16–17 – VisionDive, Vincent Legrand, VectorVicePhoto. 18–19 – Tommy Daynjer, GKIps, s.dali. 20–21 – Vera NewSib, Rich Carey. 22–23 – Rich Carey, Denis Moskvinov.

CONTENTS

Page 4	Habitats Around the World
Page 6	Ocean Climate
Page 8	Ocean Life
Page 12	Sea Turtles
Page 14	Dolphins
Page 16	Great White Sharks
Page 18	Life Cycles
Page 20	Protect the Oceans
Page 22	Our Ocean Journey
Page 24	Glossary and Index

Words that look like <u>this</u> can be found in the glossary on page 24.

HABITATS AROUND THE WORLD

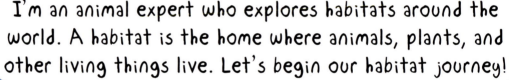

I'm an animal expert who explores habitats around the world. A habitat is the home where animals, plants, and other living things live. Let's begin our habitat journey!

Oceans are large bodies of salt water. Oceans cover most of Earth's surface. The largest ocean in the world is called the Pacific Ocean. Are you ready to start exploring?

OCEAN CLIMATE

Climate is the usual weather that happens in a place. Some oceans are warm. Some are cold. The Indian Ocean is the warmest ocean on Earth. The Arctic Ocean is the coldest.

Indian Ocean

The Antarctic Ocean is another cold ocean. The Atlantic and Pacific Oceans are the largest oceans on Earth. They are so large that different parts of them have different climates.

Would you prefer to live by the warm Indian Ocean or the freezing cold Antarctic Ocean?

Antarctic Ocean

OCEAN LIFE

The ocean is filled with <u>diverse</u> wildlife. Most ocean animals can breathe underwater. But some animals can only stay underwater for a while. Then they come up to the surface to breathe air.

Whales are <u>mammals</u>. They come above the water to breathe through their blowhole.

Can you see the water spraying out of the blowhole?

8

Millions of fish live in ocean habitats. Some types of fish, such as clownfish, only live in warm ocean habitats. Other types of fish <u>migrate</u> to warmer waters in colder months.

Pufferfish have sharp spines to protect themselves from <u>predators</u>.

The ocean is home to plant life, too. Some plants float at the surface. Others are rooted into the ocean floor. These plants provide food and shelter for ocean animals.

SEA TURTLES

Look over there! It's a sea turtle. Sea turtles are <u>reptiles</u>. They live in both cold and warm ocean habitats. Their shells help protect them from predators.

Shell

Sea turtles spend most of their lives underwater. However, they do breathe air. They can go as long as two hours without a breath of air. They spend time underwater diving for food.

DOLPHINS

Wow, there's a dolphin! The dolphin is hunting by using echolocation. It makes a clicking sound. The sound moves through the water until it hits something. Then that sound travels back to the dolphin. This process tells the dolphin where its <u>prey</u> is.

14

Dolphins have better eyesight than humans. This helps them hunt for food. It also helps them watch out for predators, such as sharks.

Look at how they jump out of the water.

GREAT WHITE SHARKS

Great white sharks are some of the world's largest predators. They are found in warm oceans all over the planet.

Great white sharks can also be found in cold waters. They have <u>adapted</u> to keep their bodies warm in low <u>temperatures</u>. This helps their muscles stay strong and makes it easier for them to swim fast to catch fish.

Great white sharks have 300 sharp teeth. Don't get too close!

LIFE CYCLES

Life cycles are the different stages a living thing goes through. Sea turtles lay eggs on beaches in nests. Then the eggs hatch. The babies crawl to the ocean. This journey can be dangerous. Many animals, such as birds and crabs, eat the newborn turtles before they reach the water.

If you find a baby sea turtle, do not touch it!

The babies that reach the ocean grow into adult turtles. Some of these turtles will lay their own eggs one day. The life cycle of sea turtles continues.

Only about 1 in 1,000 baby sea turtles makes it to adulthood.

PROTECT THE OCEANS

Baby sea turtles sometimes crawl through garbage to make it to the ocean. This litter is dangerous to sea turtles and other ocean life. People must throw away their trash instead of littering.

Ocean animals are losing their homes because of people. We must stop it!

One of the biggest threats to the ocean is garbage. Garbage harms animals and damages habitats. People can <u>recycle</u> to help stop trash from going into the oceans.

OUR OCEAN JOURNEY

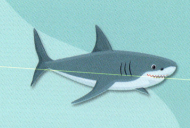

What a journey! Ocean habitats are the biggest habitats on Earth. They are home to millions of living things. Much of the ocean is unexplored. There is much more to discover.

Ocean habitats are important for many reasons. They need to be protected if we want to keep exploring their secrets. Protecting the oceans will help you have your own adventure one day.

GLOSSARY

adapted	changed over time to improve the chances of survival
diverse	different kinds
mammals	animals that are warm blooded, have a backbone, and produce milk to feed their children
migrate	to move from one place to another
predators	animals that hunt other animals for food
prey	animals that are hunted by other animals for food
recycle	use something again to make something else
reptiles	cold-blooded animals with scales
temperatures	how hot or cold things are

INDEX

blowholes 8
coral reefs 11
echolocation 14
eggs 18–19
litter 20
muscles 17
sharks 15–17
spines 9